BORN
in
FEAR

BORN in FEAR

You have the power to transform your wounds to wisdom

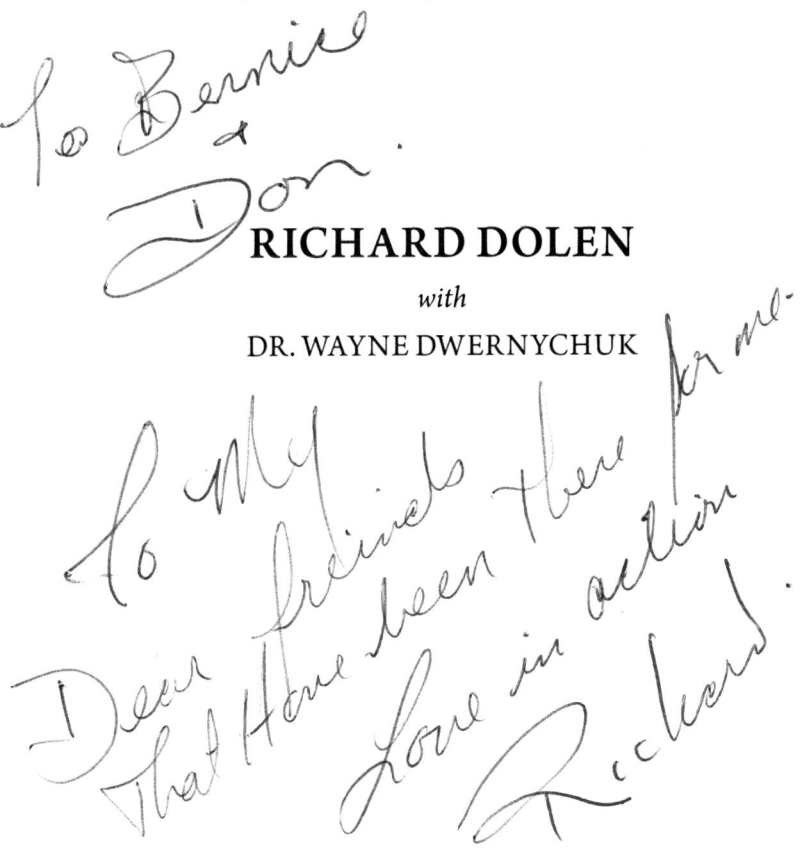

To Bernie & Don.

To My Dear freinds
That Have been there for me-
Love in action
Richard.

RICHARD DOLEN

with

DR. WAYNE DWERNYCHUK

FriesenPress

Suite 300 - 990 Fort St
Victoria, BC, V8V 3K2
Canada

www.friesenpress.com

Copyright © 2018 by Richard Dolen
First Edition — 2018

Tree of Life Image on Front Cover
Named:
TRANSFORMATION

Image Copyright Holder: Dr. Wayne Dwernychuk

Front Cover Illustrator: Wilbur J. Johnson
TSTI CYBER SOLUTIONS
Richmond, VA, USA

ISBN
978-1-5255-2371-7 (Hardcover)
978-1-5255-2372-4 (Paperback)
978-1-5255-2373-1 (eBook)

1. SELF-HELP, PERSONAL GROWTH, HAPPINESS

Distributed to the trade by The Ingram Book Company

Table of Contents

BORN in FEAR

Book Reviews

Written from the heart, and intending to help all who struggle with their past, *BORN in FEAR* is much more than inspiring. As Richard shares powerful personal stories, he simplifies complex thoughts on the relationship of fear and belief systems, while tugging on the emotions of any reader. After enduring enormous disadvantages and challenges throughout his young life, Richard has earned the strength to now share his story with us. Within his open and sincere sharing of real-life survival, he provides much useful advice, relevant to all, as we each struggle to navigate this crazy life, chasing our desire to be fighters and survivors, while resisting the pressure to cave into a pattern of victim-attitude. This is a deeply emotional writing. Nice work Mr. Dolen. Thank you.
- *Charles Lammers, Professional Book Reviewer/ Editor/Publishing Partner, Waldorf Publishing, Grapevine, Texas*

Richard Dolen is loved by many. Why so magnetic? Probably because he lives and loves with rare authenticity and generosity of heart. Deep down inside we all long to do the same.

What is it Richard loves? People, animals, places, art, music, singing, gardening, walking, spirituality, dreams, all experiences, because every experience is a teacher, once we reframe so.

With deepest concern, and little or no drama, Richard invites us to embrace our personal truths. He bids us to look at our traumatic experiences, those we have sublimated, minimized or denied and squandered so much energy repressing in order to live and be loved. Why? Because when we choose to examine our fears and self-imposed limitations we allow ourselves to truly experience freedom and love.

There is great wisdom in this book. As a Metis, two-spirited healer Richard's insights are gifts from the spirit and the divine. They are imparted with the deepest levels of caring and concern. With a heart as big as his body, he helps us accept we are loveable in spite of horrendous, hurtful or shaming childhoods or later life encounters. He reassures us and we can face our fears and grow emotionally at any age.

I am truly grateful for Richard's knowing intelligence, kindness, courage, compassion and holistic connectedness. His journey through life has been fraught with the highs and lows that have taught humility, self-searching, wonder, the power of community caring and the liberation of love - love for self, others, and fidelity to life's purpose.

It is no accident that you hold this book. The words will welcome you home.

- Mary Stacey, M.A. (Educational Administration and Policy Development), Post-Graduate Diploma (Education), B.A. (Honours, Social and Public Administration)

BORN in FEAR is truly a collection of compelling testimonies. The personal narratives contained within its pages are poignant, (all too) familiar and ultimately redemptive. The author's journey, in fact, may be the most inspirational. His journey through childhood trauma, organized religion and thwarted/then triumphant attempts at wholeness have all fed the development of his straightforward approach to transforming painful experiences into powerful life lessons... a brilliant example of the resilience of the human spirit.

- Djola Branner, B.A., M.A., M.F.A., Author, Professor of Theater, Hampshire College, Amherst, MASS.; previous positions include teacher of dance, acting, and dramatic writing at Macalester College, University of Minnesota, American Musical and Dramatic Academy, and Stanford University

BORN in FEAR is a raw, emotional journey through the deepest, darkest corners of dysfunction, abuse, judgement and victimization and through its brutally honest and heartfelt experiences, we are taken through the desperation of a lost soul looking for acceptance and a place of belonging and purpose. In its naked truths, Richard exemplifies the power of love and its ability to change the world around us by creating a holistic, loving environment that nurtures our own being to whatever shape we want our selves to be. It is a story of devastation, confusion, mistrust and above all hope. Hope and attainability of light and omnipotent love ... this is Richard Dolan's story ... this is the story of Love.

- Rita V. Arcand, Bachelor Degree in Social Work, Registered Social Worker, Certified Addiction Counsellor

Richard wrote this book to help you move forward to a happy and healthy life. By sharing his journey and the stories of people who have taken a chance and joined him in healing circles, Richard believes that doors will open and you will see the possibilities you could create in your life. It is, also, his dream that this book will help you move from a place of self-hatred to a place of self-love. It is only when we can love and accept ourselves that we can truly do the same for others. May your journey be gentle and may you be open to finding the people in your life who will support you in love and honesty.

- Peggy Chick, Life Skills Coach, Educator

PREFACE

Individuals, families, and communities can be destroyed by suicide, addiction, abuse, drugs, alcohol, violence, and many of the other social ills we face today. Through many years of working with people who aspired to change their lives, I have developed many unique and proven approaches and techniques to help them improve their situation.

My book presents an easy-to-read self-help approach to examining your life and making life-altering decisions to re-direct your future down a more positive and constructive path. I have worked in many communities in Canada and the US, and I believe that many people plagued by toxic attitudes and habits will find benefit and hope in my words.

This book serves as a reminder to those who wanted to improve their lives and did so, a reminder of where they were, where they want to go, and how to remain on their path of empowerment and positive thinking. Casting off the impulses, habits, and negative thinking of a damaged life (physically and emotionally) can be a monumental challenge. However, with the help of my words and constructive suggestions, those who are serious about change can achieve a higher quality, more satisfying life.

The book outlines how we develop certain thought processes early in life that can be destructive and carried on into adulthood. It provides examples of people whose lives have changed significantly by attending my workshops and applying my methods. This book gives confidence to those whose lives are mired in self-doubt, shame, and hopelessness.

Born in Fear will provide optimism, direction, and insight into your life, giving you a vision for a better life than the life that has, for years, caused so much pain, anguish, and regret. I wrote this book to help readers move forward and enter a happy, healthy life by sharing my journey and the stories of people who have taken a chance and joined me in healing circles and workshops. Through reading this book, I believe that doors will open, and you will see the possibilities you can create in your life. It is also my dream that this book will help you move from a place of self-hatred to a place of self-love. May your journey be as gentle as possible, and may you be open to finding the people in your life who will support you in love and honesty. Our society is plagued with physical and emotional turmoil. Understanding how you can lift yourself out of the grasp of depression, addiction, and violence will help you escape such self-abuse permanently. The work we do is performed with integrity and knowing that only good comes as a result of attendance and commitment. We share a global thought that, if we are willing, anything is possible.

By way of encouragement, here are some testimonies from people who have attended my workshops.

> "This program has brought me to the greatest understanding as to who I am, why I was the way I was, what was stopping me, and what I am capable of. I have found that I am capable of love and kindness."
> —Ken

> "This program really opened my eyes. It showed me how much I was missing out on life."
> —Eleanor

> "This program was good for me, because I came from being angry and abusive to being a gentle and kinder person. This program taught me to be a good person and a good role model."
> —Charlie

> "Communities that utilize this program will benefit from it, because it offers an effective outlook on how to go on

with life in a positive and healthy way. It worked for me, because I was so stuck being the victim of childhood trauma that it prevented me from leading a healthy and productive life."
—Linda

And so, the healing begins.

ACKNOWLEDGEMENTS

I dedicate this book to the memory of my partner of twenty-four years, Lawrence Duckett. Lawrence loved me without condition, as I loved him. He taught me how to live without shame, fear, or guilt. Lawrence passed away on April 28, 2013. He was only fifty-seven years old. I will miss him to my last breath.

My gratitude . . . first to my creator, then to all the people who participated in every workshop and training program I have ever done. Thank you for teaching me.

Gratitude to my soul sisters, Lillian Bigstone (Jackson), Brenda Bigchild, and Jean Anderson, and for their unwavering support and love.

Gratitude to my favourite and dearest cousin, Sandra Hall, for saving my life and teaching (allowing) me to *be* me for the first time in my life. With love and kindness.

Gratitude to my nephew, Jason, who stood by me during the most difficult days of my life. Thank you, and I love you.

Gratitude to my brother, Don, who took my hand and loved me without judgement and continues to support me during my down times.

Gratitude to my mom and dad for bringing me into this world and doing their very best . . . thank you.

Gratitude to my grade nine teacher, Jan Truss, who saw the best in me even when I couldn't . . . thank you.

Gratitude to my neighbours near all my homes. Thank you for being part of my life and supporting me.

Gratitude to all my friends, who unflinchingly stepped up to the plate when I needed them . . . thank you.

Gratitude to my friend, Harold Neden, who, without the slightest hesitation, offered generosity at a level I never thought possible. Thank you for loving me.

Gratitude to Mary Stacey and her family, Jessy, Kerry, and Aaron. Thank you for a kind of love that doesn't come one's way often.

Gratitude to Leslie Joy for her sincere support and generosity, along with her dear husband, Dr. Wayne Dwernychuk. Without hesitation, they helped me pick up the many pieces of my life following Lawrence's passing. They sat with me brainstorming and assisting me in making this book a reality. For all this, including typing the drafts, editing, reading my hen scratch, offering suggestions for the book, humour, and great meals, I humbly thank you both.

Gratitude to my friends, Peter and Kat Weyly, for believing in me and loving me. Peter passed away recently. His humour and booming voice are sorely missed.

Gratitude to the oh so many, too many to mention, who have touched my heart . . . I thank you.

Gratitude to all the children in the world who trust us "big people." God bless you all.

Gratitude to Diva and Madge for taking me on long walks in the woods, for letting me cry and scream, and for licking my hand and letting me know they were there. You two dogs have heard it all.

CHAPTER 1

UNCONSCIOUS WOUNDS

Don't let your wounds make you become someone you're not.
—Demi Moore

Most of us do not wish to admit that we may have been wounded by experiences in our lives. This sounds somewhat harsh, and it says we are not okay. It also implies something is wrong with us. We have spent our lives making sure that all is right in our world. This is why we stay "unconscious."

For this book to make a difference in your life, the most important factor is your willingness to be honest on a level that most of us do not wish to experience. However, living life to the fullest demands honesty. This does not mean being honest to the entire world, only to yourself. ("To thine own self be true.") I mean real honesty, deep honesty, honesty that breaks the rules of pretence and denial.

A friend of mine, whom we will call Spencer, and three others were brainstorming about this book. He is over sixty years old. As a child, he watched his father beat his mother many times after drinking, attack her with a knife, and threaten to kill her with a rifle. He also saw his mom's blood splattered on the floor and his father trying to strangle her. Spencer indicated it never really affected him much, only that he would become withdrawn and silent. After working it through with the rest of us, he recognized that he had shut off his emotions, so he would not feel the pain. He was only three or four years old at that time, and this has played a role in all his adult life, including parenting, relationships, and work. He didn't fail; he simply didn't feel. What a shame.

He became a very successful man, travelling the world doing amazing things, touching the lives of thousands of people, all without emotion, maintaining the pretence that all was well. However, all was not well. Finally, suicide appeared to be the only option. He requested ECT (electro-convulsive therapy or "shock treatment") and was diagnosed with MDD (Major Depressive Disorder). One more attempt was made to select the "right" medication prior to ECT. His doctor recommended one additional drug, and it worked, preventing suicide in the nick of time. Then Spencer was able to look objectively at his life and open himself to increasing awareness and his sense of freedom. I can only imagine what he could have accomplished if emotion and wholeness had entered his life at a much earlier age. His life experiences would have undoubtedly been more fulfilling. The realization of where he came from may open new doors for Spencer.

When we make choices from ages one to four, we are unable to think through our decision-making process. We make life-forming decisions out of fear, pain, sadness, and the need to survive. What we see, hear, and feel initially is not experienced. As a result, it stays inside us, hidden and buried. In time, this state of being becomes the way we live day to day. Out of this hidden place, many things come into our adult world. Some people, like Spencer, become overachievers, unconsciously thinking, "If I am really successful and work exceptionally hard, someone will see my goodness and not see the real me." It does not have to be Dad beating Mom. It may be a multitude of events in a child's life.

If you think about how vulnerable you were as a child and how easily you could be affected by traumatic events, it does not take much for you to shift your perceptions and emotional reactions. For example, being party to yelling may cause you not to listen. More yelling may result in a child hearing the yelling but having no idea of what is being said. As you proceed in life, and someone yells at you, you may become angry or turn it inward, diminishing your self-esteem with every yelling event. As more people yell at you, you are eventually taken to a place where you may settle for less and never know why. Consequently, this unconscious reaction and decision to "not hear" as a child may stay with you for the rest of your life . . . unless you become conscious.

If we become aware of the wounds that have occurred in our lives and see them as lessons and eventually tools to help us achieve wisdom, will we experience freedom? If everyone takes the time required and experiences this as part of their journey, will they experience freedom? I can practically guarantee they will, and so will you. The clearer you are about *you*, the clearer and more in focus freedom becomes.

You will inevitably have to give up some lifelong beliefs and change some of the rules you lived by, so this could be tough. However, you must ask yourself, "How badly do I want to express *me* and experience freedom?" You will backslide. I know this for sure, as it is easy to slip back into familiar ways of being. Then you may justify why you slipped back and possibly blame someone else. Be honest, and you can "right" yourself again. Take a deep breath, and move on. If necessary, try again and again. You are worth it, and you deserve to experience and express freedom and peace. If there has been, or is, abuse in your life, and you feel stuck, accept this as only the "child's" programming. You are not stuck. Just make a new decision from an adult stance. "I desire to be loved respectfully, and . . . (you fill in the blank)." Now *you* are the one who decides if you are going to experience freedom.

If you begin to shift toward a new way of being, don't expect an abundance of support from some of the people in your life, as they may also have made childhood decisions about their lives. Most people fight change and are willing to settle for less rather than stir the pot. Remember, this is your journey, and you are not doing it to hurt anyone. Your journey may be directed at stopping the hurt. Some people say it is a never-ending job. They are wrong. If you and your friends celebrate any shift, it is not a job but a joy.

As a child, many limits were placed on me regarding family, church, other people, and so on. My mom worried about what others thought. She instilled a fear in me of almost everything. She was a master manipulator and could cut my heart with a single word stroke, such as, "You never really wanted to be part of this family anyway." Ouch! "You were supposed to be a girl." Ouch!

My dad was living outside his dream because of his beliefs and rules. He would drink on weekends. If I caught him before he got drunk, I would get a glimpse of who he really was. Mostly, however, he was silent and never showed affection. He did express one emotion though: anger.

Our home was permeated with secrets. No one spoke the truth. Consequently, leaving the family and attempting to create a new family was exceptionally difficult because of my beliefs ("Blood is thicker than water," "The family that prays together, stays together," "You can only count on family," "God says honour thy father and mother," and "How dare you to not obey the rules?")

Every time I slid back, I would see more clearly that if I stayed enmeshed in my family's rules and beliefs, I would never find freedom. I started asking myself what my fears were, how real they were, and how long was I prepared to keep giving and settling for less. Freedom was my choice, and the only way I could achieve it was to give up fear . . . unreal fear. Every once in a while, I still backslid, but not so far that I could not jump quickly back into reality.

Many of us did not have positive role models to set examples for the journey to freedom. Therefore, we have to get there *now* to provide positive role models for our children. If we live in freedom, a few will want to come along for the dance.

When a dear friend of mine became aware I was writing this book, she expressed a strong desire to tell her story. It is a story of horror, tragedy, and extreme abuse. She is a survivor through honesty and an overwhelming desire to change her life for the better. She wants to encourage others to face their demons and lift themselves out of their individual hell, to find peace and a better way to live. I present her story of pain, hope, and success as an example of emotional re-birth in the face of unbelievable odds.

> My name is Hope. I am forty-five years old, and today, I finally understand the meaning of *living* life. I say this, because for the first forty-four years, I only survived. I existed in a world of humiliation and incest, of sexual, emotional, and physical abuse that began as early as I can

recall. Through it all, I kept thinking that life could be different, but I had no knowledge of how to get there. There didn't seem to be any hope. In fact, I didn't even know what hope looked like or felt like.

I am a Cree Nation member, born and raised in a small community in northern Alberta. I am the second oldest of ten children. My mother went to residential school, and my dad worked for a residential school. As a second-generation member of the residential school system, I suffered the impacts in my upbringing. I grew up in a loveless, abusive family. As a toddler, I don't remember bonding or connecting with my mother, nor did I feel nurtured. I felt disconnected and a stranger to everyone I encountered. My world consisted of humiliation, constant put-downs, emotional abuse, and hard physical labour. I became a mother to my siblings, and at age eight, I changed diapers, scrubbed floors, washed clothes, and was tasked with constant babysitting. School became a safe haven for me, and I excelled academically.

At age five, I was raped for the first time by a neighbour, who lived across the road from us. This was the beginning of years of sexual abuse by "upstanding" members of my community, as well as my own family. I don't recall much sleep for the first eighteen years of my life, as the violations to my body and spirit continued night after night and year after year. I became silent, powerless, and didn't trust anyone, not even my parents, who were supposed to love and protect me. I never learned how to play like other children. At age five, I decided that if I was silent and small, no one would notice me. All I knew was survival. I lived in my bedroom and only came out to cook and clean or do whatever was demanded of me, even if that meant having someone pour, believe it or not, a shit pail over my head. Each night I was attacked and ter-rorized. I survived by learning to numb my senses and silence my screams, so I would not feel the physical and emotional pain.

My first recollection of wanting to die was around age ten. From then on, I continuously contemplated suicide. I decided life was too difficult, and death appeared to be the only way out.

At age sixteen, I made my first serious attempt by over-dosing on pills and ended up in the hospital. Due to the questionable wisdom of the social system, that was my first introduction to psychiatric care and antidepressants. One month later, I was released from the hospital, but nothing changed at home. The abuse continued, as did my powerlessness and desperation, leading me to self-mutilation. Seeing blood ooze from my body and feeling no pain became an obsession. I was a "pro" at leaving my body.

I left home at age eighteen and married an officer from the law-enforcement community, hoping life would get better. It didn't. He beat me regularly when drinking.

In my mid-twenties, I committed to regular use of anti-depressants and talk therapy. When I look back at my years of being on meds and in psychiatric care, I realize this approach only perpetuated the cycle. Sure, I talked about the abuse, but I never got to the core of the issue and addressed my real feelings. The hour would be up, and I would be on my four-hour trip home, reeling from the emotional triggers that had come up during the session. I would be crying so hard that I couldn't see the road and would have to pull over to vomit as I tried to gather enough strength to continue my travels. The bodily sensations and the odours of sexual abuse that were front and centre during the abuse were unbearable. All the while at home I focused every ounce of my energy trying to look normal, happy, and stable.

I had four children from two loveless/abusive marriages, all the while still living with a decision I had made at age four or five—to be silent, and maybe I won't be noticed. I worked and functioned, knowing I had to feed my children three times a day. As a child, I vowed I would never raise my children as I was raised . . . without nurturing and love. But there I was, doing just that, taking more and more antidepressants to mask everything, to cope, and, most of all, to stay sane. However, the silent voice inside me continued to say that life had to be better than this.

Then one day "hope" appeared in the form of an invitation to a facilitator training program. At the time, I saw it as an opportunity to enhance my skills. Little did I know it would give me back my life. The training program, called Turning Wounds to Wisdom, is exactly that, a program that takes you out of your pain and elevates you to your greatness. It is the most unbelievable approach to healing that you can imagine. It provided me with a safe, secure, and loving place to deal with my past hurts, humiliation, and abuse.

After having written off men forever, I found safety in Richard Dolen, founder and facilitator of this training program. Richard is a man with an amazing gift for bringing anyone to their greatness, to be the best they can be. His guidance provides people with an ability to walk in the light of love and hope. I trusted him with my life. There were no clocks or textbook agendas, and in ten weeks, the process did for me what twenty-one years of counselling and medications had failed to do. It taught me to deal with my issues, to become a powerful woman, and, most of all, to love myself.

Today, my life is full of new awareness. I live each day knowing that I can overcome any problem by making conscious adult decisions regarding my life. A few weeks prior to graduation from Turning Wounds to Wisdom, I became antidepressant free and stopped self-mutilation. After shutting down for over forty years, I am finally capable of feeling, both physically and emotionally. I am able to love myself, I can feel love, and I can love back. I know I am worth it and that it is not too late to become the parent I always wanted my children to have. I feel powerful, confident, and will not settle for less. Life *can* be different. Life *can* be good.

There are so many people out there living in abuse and terror. I am telling my story, because I want them to know that hope *is* available. I want them to know what that hope looks like.

Hope is a survivor. She chose to face and overcome her wounds and fears, thus fostering a better life.

At this point, you may not know or understand the wounds and scars you have suffered. The pain in your life may be overwhelming. Dare to step toward the edge . . . and move forward.

CHAPTER 2

UNCONSCIOUS DECISIONS

Your life is determined by the sum of the choices that YOU make.
—Frank Sonnenberg

What did you learn between the ages of one and five, and what and how did you make decisions at that age that affected you for the rest of your life? Here is an example to get you thinking.

A boy grew up in a home with no siblings. His mom was an educator, and his dad worked as a skilled labourer. Dad came home drunk and beat Mom . . . Mom screamed. The boy was a witness to these frequent scenes of violence. I asked him as an adult what decisions he made as a child when he saw his dad beating his mom.

"I didn't make any decisions," he said. "I was just a small boy." So, I asked him how he felt, he said "Fear, just plain terror."

"Well, at least you had feelings and emotions," I replied. "So, what decisions did you make based on those emotions?"

"I couldn't do anything about the violence," he said. "I couldn't change it. I was too small and not strong enough to intervene, so I hid and became silent."

"So, could that have been the decision you made, to become silent because you couldn't change things?"

"Maybe," he replied.

"How do you live out this childhood decision in your adult life?"

He shook his head. "I don't."

I pointed out that he was brilliant, had become a doctor, but he never felt comfortable taking the lead, as in being the sole owner of a business.

"I just knew I couldn't do it," he replied without hesitation, the same statement he had made as a child.

It took some work for him to see the possibility that maybe he was living with a child's decision. Now conscious of that, as an adult, he can make new decisions based on knowledge. People in his life can better understand how and why he "checked out" at certain times in his life. As a consequence, his relationships can become healthier, given that he now understands that almost everyone he knows is probably living out childhood decisions.

I think about the decisions I made as a child and am amazed at how they have played out in my life. For example, my dad would consistently say to me, "How many times do I have to tell you . . . are you that dumb?" The decision for me was that I must be "dumb," because I couldn't understand what he wanted. I was hearing impaired and dyslexic; consequently, I guessed at most things and became vulnerable to suggestions made by other people, who were bigger and smarter. "Don't talk back" kept me silent for most of my life. "You're not as smart as you think you are" kept me guessing most of the time. If anyone told me to "Do it this way," I wouldn't question it. After all, I was dumb. All this because I wasn't smart enough to make any big decisions.

Mom compared us with each other and with others in the community/world. "Eat your food; there are starving kids out there . . . you don't know how lucky you are." I relinquished my "power" when I was very young and could not see myself as smart, capable, nice looking, loveable, or even capable of matching up to others. I carried all these decisions into my adult life, where I raised children and entered relationships, but I couldn't keep a job. Eventually, after starting my own business, I became successful, but I still couldn't see myself as successful.

Then, through a lot of hard work and the help of some amazing people, I woke up. Thank you, thank you. Now I try to make decisions from an adult perspective. I had to surrender the need to be right about those childhood decisions. That was tough, considering I had convinced myself I was not worthy, not smart enough, or just plain stupid in almost every facet of life.

Cathy is a schoolteacher and, in my estimation, a very good one. She feels safe around children and is skilled at teaching them. However, she keeps her guard up when it comes to family and other adults, even her husband. He's hung in there through all the tough times. Cathy says she has been very hard on him, and he is still there. She's not sure why.

She was at one of my workshops and disclosed that, at three days old, her mom gave her up. She suspected something had happened at an early age, because she never felt loved and decided that she was unlovable. She was raised by her grandparents, calling them Mom and Dad. Cathy said her biological mom was "around" periodically but shut her out all the time. Her real mom had two boys after Cathy, and when they did family things, Cathy would not be included. Consequently, she decided at a young age that she must be bad and not good enough, and she became angry. At age twelve, her grandma passed away, and Cathy felt lost and alone. One year later, her dad (grandpa) committed suicide. She was left completely alone. Many years of trauma lay ahead of her.

My friend, Alice, was the last born of twelve children. Her mother did not want any more children and told her she was a mistake. Her mother almost died in childbirth and was sent away to a different hospital. Baby Alice was left at that hospital. She said she always felt that people would leave her, because she wasn't good enough. At birth, her mother wasn't there emotionally, and she felt abandoned. When her mom returned home with baby Alice, there was no nurturing. By age two, she decided if she worked extra hard, her mom would love her. Not so. Her mom was an angry person, even though she was not necessarily angry at Alice. At age three, Alice decided it was her fault her mom was so angry. Therefore, her next unconscious decision was to be a good little girl and try her best to keep the peace.

As an adult, she has retained the feeling of not being good enough and has gone to great lengths to retain that self-image. She has pushed people away who did, in fact, love her and paid her compliments, and she has continued to struggle in relationships. She has even "created" rheumatoid arthritis, which can be a product of being hard and rigid and not allowing yourself to make mistakes.

Her childhood decisions regarding not being good enough, coupled with her mother's voice of "You will never be good enough," continue to echo in her mind, overriding any positive compliments or love from others.

Alice attended university and became a health-care provider—a very good one. She is still trying to keep the peace, work hard, and be a "good girl." After attending a few workshops with me, she was able to bring all her hidden feelings into full consciousness and start to make new adult decisions regarding how she wants to be. She has come a long way in a short time and continues to be an amazing health-care provider, only now she is not out to save the world to but use her gift in a more powerful manner.

It always surprises me when I see people make shifts after daring to be honest about what happened in their lives. The only way to shift is to be brutally honest and to work through the process with some help. One person said to me, "I had no idea that freedom was so close."

CHAPTER 3

BORN IN FEAR

*You gain strength, courage, and confidence by every experience
in which you really stop to look fear in the face. You must do the thing
which you think you cannot do.*
—Eleanor Roosevelt

Anyone who says, "I'm not afraid of anyone or anything" is living in great fear. "Be good and follow the rules, and you will have nothing to fear." This person is also living in fear. "I can't do anything about it anyway." More fear. Fighting and arguing is a nice little bunch of fear. What causes a fight or an argument: the need to be right or fear of being wrong?

We have been taught and encouraged to think that fear is a weakness. Therefore, denial of fear allows it to grow and fester inside. Never letting anyone know you are afraid keeps the secret and may create illness.

Where does fear come from? Parents use fear to keep children in check, not that they do so consciously. Churches teach fear of God. If you do anything counter to the church's rules, you are told that hell awaits. Bad and good . . . which is which . . . I'm not sure.

I was raised Roman Catholic, so shame, guilt, and fear were my foundation at an early age. This is a difficult one to get around, especially when the Church has most of the money and won't share. My family was well below the poverty line, and watching my father place scarce money in the collection plate disturbed me to no end. That is what my father was taught, so he followed the tradition. It wasn't his intention to do harm; he simply did what he thought was right. I became an altar boy, so I could steal the money back!

I now believe that if the Church teaches "only" love with no judgments and fear, I may go back. I simply do not see this happening. There would be a loss of control of the masses, and that would not suit the Church's objectives. Think about the wars that are waged because of religion, greed, and control. I am sure that hell would be my final residence in *every* religion, given I would never buy hate.

Schools are another teacher of fear. First, we are told we must attend, or we will never be successful. If a child struggles to understand the curriculum, whether someone says anything or not, the child decides that he or she may not make the cut. Fear sets in, in the form of low self-esteem. Think about it. We send our children away to school at age six or less, where they are made to follow the rules of strangers, thus instilling fear if they break those rules. Children spend an entire day being programmed to follow a set of rules, and if they don't, they may get in trouble or reported to Mom and Dad, who now become advocates for the teacher, thus instilling another level of fear. No adult I know would put up with what we ask of our children, such as asking in front of their peers if they can go pee.

Most parents are trying to do their best to make money, so their children receive all the extras, but often they never get to see how their children are really doing. Most children know their parents work hard, so they simply follow the rules. But really, how happy are they? Education is a big deal. I was once told by a very clever person that it only takes twelve years to brainwash someone. Think about our young people and how they are driven to achieve and get more education, so they can get a good job, work hard, make money, and, ultimately, put their babies back into the system.

I know some excellent teachers who care about their students, but they must follow the rules of the system. Not much room for fun in that. But one must remember, this is a job for them, and to keep it they have to agree to follow the rules. At the day's end, the children go home with homework that must be done. Parents then become the teacher, and they are not usually great at this task. Most adults would not come home from work and then do their job for another hour or so, like we force our children to do. Rules are made for control and order, not for fun or to create happiness.

If fear has nothing to oppose, it will disappear. How would you like it if there was no fear? Most of our fear was taught to us during our childhood by parents, teachers, doctors, clergy, friends, and news of what was going on in the world. Fear is a habitual pattern initiated in early childhood. We live in and around fear for so long and are not allowed to talk about it. Fear infiltrates our psyche and becomes part and parcel of our story and how we respond to the world. We pretend everything is great, because fear has become part of who we are. Many people, by the time they are grown, don't recognize their fears and live around them until they get old and die.

To flip fear, you must first recognize it and be honest about its presence. Tell the truth about where fear comes from. What happened to instil this fear? You must break its hold on you piece by piece. You have to want fear to stop, so you can know the other side of it. For me, this is happening now.

Angela's fear started when she was a small child. She was born to a mother who was born in fear and settled for less her entire life. She married a man who drank and became mean and violent to the children. By the time Angela was nine years old, she already believed she was only good for having babies. Her mother told her and showed her that was her purpose. Being educated and successful was never in the equation. Her mother stayed for the children. She said she was too afraid to leave, to change, so she accepted a lie: "That's how life is."

Angela's dad would hit her mom, and her mother would faint, causing Angela to believe her mother was dying. She would go into total fear, hiding under a blanket as her dad continued to hit her mom. Sometimes she and her mom would leave the house and hide before her dad came home. Her mom would set up a little camp and tell Angela to keep quiet until he passed out. Angela says she is stuck in her childhood because of her fear to speak about the violence that took place.

Angela remembers a time when even her uncle (her dad's brother) beat her mom, and her dad did absolutely nothing. Her mom was always in fear and guilt until her untimely death of cancer at the young age of seventy-two.

Angela also remembers a time when she and her brother had impetigo all over their bodies. Her dad forced her mom to drive him and his friend to the US for five days. Angela was to look after the children, but she fell sick and went to bed. The seeping wounds caused her to stick to the bedsheets. Her brother had to cut her away from the sheets, just prior to her going to the hospital for help.

Now, as an adult with eight children, she moves into overwhelming fear when one of her children becomes ill. She fears something bad is going to happen. Her guilt and fear have fostered an obsession regarding cleanliness. She also finds it difficult to enjoy anything because of her fears.

Angela says she instilled fear in her children, and now they simply survive instead of live. When she witnessed the lives of her children, she did not want to admit she was responsible for where they were in life. She became depressed and hopeless. Then one day when she was near the "bottom," she became aware of one of my workshops and decided to attend. That's when I met Angela, and she says it was then her life took a sharp turn for the better. What she experienced meant she would have to start facing and owning her fears. This is not an easy task for anyone.

The abuse and hopelessness trapped her in a dead-end relationship. Her siblings also lived in fear, so they were adept at sucking each other into the vortex of fear, keeping the secrets regarding their childhood and the sexual abuse, the put-downs that left deep wounds, parental absenteeism, family violence, booze, sexual deviance, and so on. She learned that if she stayed in fear, she could always blame others for her shortcomings. Angela said she had lied her entire life just to feel a "little" okay. That was better than nothing.

Angela's children filled the void for a while and helped her keep her head in the sand. Consequently, it was time for her to move on. She was missing the moment . . . the present.

She decided that was not how she wanted to live. The workshop Angela experienced with me opened her eyes. She had to be honest. At times, the experience was harsh. However, she stuck it out and started living with less fear and living in the moment. I told Angela she was creating her life out of the spectre of fear, and I challenged her to try something different.

In a month, Angela had a job, a home for her children, and a car. She was ecstatic about what she had created. Over time, she kept moving ahead: a better job, a better car, more happiness, and a new relationship. However, old fears raised their heads, and she had a difficult time accepting life could be that good forever. The relationship became abusive. She lost her job. Her children began talking back to her. At one point, Angela blamed me for instilling what she interpreted as unrealistic expectations for her life.

Letting go again and again, she is well on her way. However, the familiar keeps calling. As a result, Angela must keep it in check.

When we live in fear, either consciously or unconsciously, one thing leads to another, and if we don't figure it out, something or someone else will, such as sickness or disease. A doctor can prescribe medications that may help if you wish to stay numb. The longer you remain in fear, the longer it will take to escape fear's chains and feel joy and happiness.

I have met so many people living in a false sense of happiness, pretending that everything is fine. They make statements like, "A good argument is healthy," "You can't expect to be happy all the time," "It all works itself out," "No sense in complaining," and "I can't change it anyway."

We are born in fear, whether we accept it or not. We carry on old teachings and beliefs and hope our children will be happier than we were. But the voice inside keeps saying, "Is this all there is striving to 'be' and to 'get,' and then we die?"

At my partner's funeral in California, many of his old friends attended. They had all spent time growing up and hanging out. They used to talk of dreams and wishes. One lady said Lawrence was the only one of the group to step out of his fears and travel the world. We all dreamed it and promised we would, she said, but fear kept us here, not going anywhere of consequence.

To escape fear, you must own it and name it. Truth is the beginning of freedom, and realizing where the fear comes from is another important step. We must seriously look at what we give up to stay in the relative safety of fear. When you can recognize and identify what fear has done to your life, you are taking a huge step forward.

Fear keeps you from taking risks. I'm not talking about sky diving or bungee jumping. I'm talking about your happiness. Dare you risk loss of friends, family, and dead-end jobs? Are you willing to try new ways of doing and being? Are you willing to risk a short solo journey? The future is limitless . . . if you let go of fear.

Many things have been said and written about fear and how to change it. I am not sure there is a quick fix. My hope in writing this book is that perhaps some new doors will open for those who read it. The old tapes and the familiar will always be close at hand. As a result, you may slide back into your old false sense of safety whenever you wish. Don't do it!

There will be friends and family who do not want you to be free of fear. They will offer a multitude of reasons for why you should stay the way you are. They will try to convince you that you are not in fear and that it is okay to keep old secrets, especially about the family. You may encounter numerous hidden traps.

Everyone lives with their fear in their own way. That is why fear is so difficult to stop. Please, do not wait until your children are grown, until you cannot afford it, or until you are too old to choose happiness. Do not give up anything. The cost to stay in fear is monumental. Make a list of what it may cost, such as your dream job, a desired relationship, your health, travel, and so on. The payoff for remaining in fear never outweighs the cost; it is the opposite of what you desire. Fear may seem like a friend, but it works in tandem with your ego and is, effectively, your most dangerous enemy. Love of self and others counters fear and eventually wins.

CHAPTER 4

OLD TAPES

Real freedom is creative, proactive, and will take me into new territories.
I am not free if my freedom is predicated on reacting to my past.
—Kenny Loggins

When we enter this world, we come perfectly whole and complete, exactly how we were meant to be. Most of our parents were happy we arrived and had great expectations for us, although they had no idea how those expectations would eventually look, given they had already been programmed in specific rules and beliefs, and they needed to be right about the future.

Parents come from different directions and try their best to keep love alive. A mom's template is made up of how women should be and what is expected of them, including how to dress, how to raise children, and cooking and taking care of her husband. Mothers have their beliefs fixed at an early age.

A father's template has four walls and is filled with how a man should be. He must be strong (whatever that means), not express hurt or pain (he shouldn't cry, for fear of being called a sissy), and he must work hard to provide for his family.

Girls are taught to love their fathers despite all their pitfalls and be prepared to never speak of such things. They will undoubtedly become "Daddy's little girl." However, they should not expect to receive what boys receive. A boy has privileges, even though these may be hard knocks in life. Remember, you are a man.

In this formulation process, we may be hurt or damaged in so many ways. A look can instill fear; so can yelling, hitting, comparing, competing, judging, and put-downs. Schools, churches, doctors, and other authorities create a tug-of-war over our minds.

If you want to grow beyond the "taught fears," some rules or family traditions must be broken. Why? Because they limit us and prevent us from getting on the "edge" of progress. Whatever you were taught as a child in whatever way you experienced it will result in triggers or "tapes." You will react to such tapes in a manner you do not realize, like a knee-jerk reaction to some stimulus.

Overcoming these tapes and growing requires practice, practice, and more practice. One reason why this is so difficult is that your ego is now a full partner in your psyche and, essentially, runs the show. The ego is a trickster and wants you to stay in your "box" and avoid change. "Don't rock the boat . . . If it was good enough for Mom and Dad, it should be good enough for you . . . It's just the way it is . . . Don't be who you are if it doesn't fit the norm." Your ego may throw many curves at you to keep you from being all you can be. The ego has its finger on the "on" switch of your tapes.

Let's say you wish to release some anger over someone. Your ego will try to convince you that you have justifiable reasons for that anger. Similar processes will play out for judgments, hate, regrets, and old teachings and beliefs. The ego's insidiousness limits you from your untapped potential. We have been programmed to be a certain way. It depends on where your parents came from with respect to their teaching. What happens to you along the way manufactures tapes to make you feel safe, less than or better than others, shy or introverted, and aggressive or loud. The tapes also keep you following rules, remaining invisible, and prevent you from taking risks, looking for a cause, and so on. We do this because of our short history and the tapes that play in our mind.

Just writing this chapter has caused me to play old tapes, making the process very challenging:

Tape 1 . . . "You are not smart, so why are you writing this?"

Tape 2 ... "Who do you think you are, elevating yourself above others?"

Tape 3 ... "No one will read this drivel."

What should you do when this happens? Stop the tapes! Go for a walk, and recognize your ego is playing its dirty little tricks on you. It keeps playing these old tapes to keep you in your comfortable little box, which was formulated at an early age.

Don't let your ego make you angry at yourself. This is where you and the tapes require clarification as to who is in control of the "on/off" button. It must be you!

You will start recognizing the playing of tapes when you feel stuck in the past, and you can't bring yourself to move forward. The tapes will keep you in the familiar and prevent risk taking. You will tell yourself to "play it safe," and all will be okay. This will happen over and over and never move you forward, preventing you from seeing what is on the other side of the tapes and away from your ego.

I see the ego as a little muscle man sitting on my shoulder, a bully telling me what to do. When I don't listen to him, he becomes very nice. If that doesn't work, he becomes sarcastic and starts up the old tapes and won't give up. That's when I flick him off my shoulder and tell him in no uncertain terms to "fuck off." When I do this, the tapes stop, and I feel some freedom. That means freedom from fear.

A book written by Dr. Wayne Dyer, *The Sacred Self*, woke me up to the ego. It is an amazing book and helped me to recognize my ego and how it has kept me entrapped and unhealthy. That book changed my life, and I thank Dr. Dyer for enhancing my journey and rendering that change achievable.

The only way to stop the chain of events involving the ego is to break it. If you do not wish your children to play old tapes, then you must stop playing yours. These tapes keep us from living in the moment, and whether or not you like it, that's all we have right now ... the moment.

The rationale for retaining old tapes is they offer a weird sense of "normal." When you decide to stop playing your tapes, you can symbolically return them to the teachers who helped generate your tapes, or simply lay them out at a garage sale with "NO RETURNS ACCEPTED" written on them.

It is possible, but this means serious change . . . big changes in cognitive behaviours. If you wish to grow beyond your fears, sometimes you must recognize and check the triggers on your tape player. Waking up means facing your ego. This requires vigilance and forcefulness. The ego is an adept trickster, to the point of having convinced us that we actually need it to survive.

For your sake, take a stand and eliminate the ego's impact, which is such a destructive force to you and those you love. If the ego can take second place to your integrity (keeping your word to yourself), it becomes less and less in control. Your integrity becomes the frontrunner in a new way of being.

(EGO = Easing God Out or easing out that which you know inside to be right.) Love of self, knowing it and feeling it, fosters integrity. Integrity will definitely give the ego a run for its money (i.e., control).

CHAPTER 5

THE CHANGING

The only thing standing between you and your goal is the bullshit story you keep telling yourself as to why you can't achieve it.
—Jordan Belfort

You may have heard the following saying: "If you want change, you can't keep doing the same thing over and over and expect a different result."

Wishing your life to change is not good enough. You must do more than simply wish it to be so. What are your intentions? Having good intentions is very important, but, you require more than just motives. My mother used to say, "The road to hell is paved with good intentions." I think she was saying that you must have integrity and do what you intend to do.

When I think of change, it usually means that something is not working in one's life. It could be health, a relationship, adult children, work, a death, or simply unhappiness. We have been taught to accept the things we cannot change, like the weather, nature, or the colour of our eyes. However, other subjects also fit in the "I can't change" category. "If they would simply smarten up and change their ways, things would be better." Sorry, but that is not the way it works. Blame just keeps you in the same place, so you don't have to change. You can't place the onus outside yourself to effect change within. Issuing a million excuses will bring change to a grinding halt. "I'm not ready for change" means "I won't change." "I'm too old to change" means "I won't change." "That's just the way I am. If they don't like it, tough" means "It's *their* fault, and *they* should change." "I have always been this way, and it seems to work for me" means "Fuck off."

My family, church, government, and school kept me in a place of stasis by making it right to conform to the way I *thought* I should be. If you are truly happy and without fear, skip the rest of this chapter, because it will be of no use to you. If being in a familiar place is good enough for you, if you have created a false sense of security to get by and you think that's all you really need and that's all there is to life . . . great. However, if your purpose in being here is the pursuit of happiness, I challenge you to think of yourself as a vessel, perhaps like a car. You must check the "" on your level of happiness. Where does it read—full, half full, low, or zero? How happy do you wish to be? You may ask yourself this question, and if you are not where you wish to be, just standing around wringing your hands and waiting will not raise your level of happiness.

Most of us have created a "get-by syndrome." "As long as it works, sort of, all I need is to 'get by.'" To me, this means stay where you are, don't rock the boat, don't make waves, and don't upset anyone or anything. It means staying in your box—your little place on the planet, where all that you have been taught, all that you have learned, all that has happened to you, all your pain, all your joy, and all your beliefs have been assembled to create a sense of happiness and security, albeit, perhaps a false one. Really, I must ask, how happy are you, honestly? "Oh, I'm just fine. I like things the way they are." Is that really true?

I have this thing going. It's like there has to be more than just a routine that we have created to survive on this planet. The programs that tell us we are lucky, because we are not starving and not faced with war, we live in the best country . . . well, why question them? Things are the way they are, and we can't really do anything about it, so why try? Consequently, we stay the same. We continue to accept all the beliefs and rules imposed on us by our "teachers": church, school, family, government, society, friends, and so on, and, for the most part, we pretend we are happy.

For most of us, change is just a thought, an idea. Change encompasses work and risk. It does not happen on its own simply because we think it's a good idea. The reason I'm saying these words is to challenge you to check your level of happiness . . . truthfully. Most of the time when I challenge people on their level of happiness, they become defensive and wish to protect their response. Eighty percent or more are not doing their dream job. They have a job that gets them by, and they pretend it's okay and produces their "happiness."

I know many people who are in a relationship and are unhappy, and yet, they stay. Why? "For the children," they say. However, for the most part, it's a lie. They may say "I love him/her." Another lie. "We do have fun sometimes" (probably at each other's expense). "We are in counselling to make it work." (Yeah, right. One of you is in counselling, and the other is just "there"). "I've spent half my life in this relationship, and I'm not giving it up (at any cost)." What is being said with these examples is "I am afraid of change. I'm not sure enough of myself to make it on my own, so sacrificing some of my happiness is not that big a price to pay. After all, this is my third relationship, and I promised myself I would make it work."

I work with many families who are unhappy; however, they persist, go to reunions, and let Aunt Mary and Uncle Tom make fun of them. Even if it hurts, they smile. After all, it's "family." The rules around family are very scary for me. This is so, because even if you want to change, they have hundreds of reasons why you should not. What happens if you leave the family? They become fearful that the family's secrets will be revealed. They may blame you and accuse you of "writing off" the family. This approach allows the family to stay the same, to avoid change.

You change for you. If you go back, most families will not celebrate your happiness. Most will think you want to come back to the fold. If you do, then you can't change, and you get trapped into a false sense of happiness by the old definition, that which existed prior to your "change." It is one of the broadest changes you will have to make. This is not about love. You can change and make difficult choices regarding your family and continue to love them, but you don't have to be like them.

When I think about how many people I have met in my life, there are few who I can honestly say were really happy. Most of them never considered that making a change might bring them happiness. So, what is happiness, and should you be happy all the time? That is up to you. When I was married, my wife said, "I'm not a morning person, so don't talk to me until after I have my morning coffee." That is changeable, and she did change. Consequently, we started our day with a little happiness, which made a difference for our day. If just getting up with a smile and being happy can improve your day, isn't it worth it?

What else might you change that will provide you with a little more happiness? What if you didn't complain out loud or in your head all day, for possibly an entire week? Could that open the door to some happiness? I challenge you to try not complaining for two weeks, and see what happens. If the result is positive, then challenge someone else to do the same, and see if it brings you and others an elevated sense of happiness.

What if we dropped all judgments, including self-judgements? You are your own worst critic. That would mean you probably would have to break some old teachings. However, if you didn't have to make those judgments as part of your new belief system, would that bring you a little more happiness? When we judge, it is hard on our karma, and it makes us unhappy. Can you imagine how it makes the one being judged feel?

What if we became less critical toward others, including ourselves? Give yourself and others room to experiment and make some slip-ups from which you can learn. Your happiness "meter" will go up. That's what change can do for you. You need to get real and honest with your happiness. Change does not mean that the way things are is wrong. It simply means that things are not working out for you any longer. However, if things are not working out for you, and you remain in the same mind-set and expect happiness to appear out of the blue and fall into your lap . . . well, good luck with that.

A friend of mine had extreme difficulty changing the furniture in his house or even the colour of the walls. It would take him months to be able to accept the changes made. Asking him to change a habit or something else about him was out of the question. Therefore, he stayed the same for the most part and faked happiness. He has said to me on occasion that he really does not care about happiness, that he is the way he is, and that's it. What happens if you don't risk, avoid taking chances, play it safe all the time, is that you will undoubtedly die with your "music" still inside you.

Everyone interprets happiness differently. I don't mimic someone else's happiness or compare it to mine. I just know my inner self well enough to know when I have to change something to keep my happiness at a level I wish to experience.

It doesn't matter what happened to you when you were young. What matters now is, do you really want to be happy? Then perhaps you must change how you look at where you came from and re-evaluate those circumstances without blame or judgments. Stop comparing yourself to others, and make a decision about you and your intentions. This requires change, and you may need assistance to step out of the past and risk living in the present. It may not be an easy process, but I guarantee your life will improve.

It is a journey that only you can decide to pursue. Remember, it doesn't matter where you came from or where you're going. As Lau Tzu says, "The journey of a thousand miles begins with one step." This is no less true of the journey toward change.

I sincerely hope this part of my book will help you open a door and take those first steps. The journey will only be as long as it takes you. Some people take the long way when their ego steps in to affect a longer route. Change can only happen if you are willing to risk and get out of your comfort zone. It can be as quick as you wish. Do not say it is hard work. You can make it as difficult as you wish, but you can also stop and rest whenever you want and make changes, so the trek doesn't necessarily have to be difficult.

What others say about their perceptions should not reflect on your journey. When I initiated my journey, I was totally naïve. Things that had happened to me or were done to me or said to me when I was a kid didn't seem so bad until someone said they were bad. They said I should be angry and that I had been cheated. I tried it on but was unable to feel what the therapist wanted me to feel. I saw some of my history as step-ping stones, and that helped make my journey shorter and easier. Listen to your gut, and you can't go wrong. Know what real gut feelings are, then listen and sing at the top of your voice like no one is listening. In this way, you may trigger someone else's desire for change and happiness, and someone else's journey may begin.

Here is my A to Z list on how to be if you want change.

A ... ANGER. The most used and accepted feeling in the world is anger. This needs to change to ATONEMENT/ACCEPTANCE ... no more emotional wars.

B ... BLAME. As long as it's not your fault, and as long as there is a fall guy/girl, blame is a safety net (a false safety net). Blast it out, and change it to BLESSINGS.

C ... CRITICAL of ourselves and others. Be patient. You may be missing some magic, so change it to a CELEBRATION of individuality—yours and others.

D ... DENIAL. Let's just pretend this is not happening, and maybe it will go away. We need to dig into our denial and use the process for DISCOVERY.

E ... ENVY. Makes us empty and creates enemies. There is nothing in the world you can't have if you are willing to create it, and that will change it into EMPOWERMENT ... your empowerment.

F ... FEAR is used to control, to bully, to keep people from risk and change. It MAKES us sick and keeps us sick. It stops us from being all we can be. It is instilled from childhood and extends well into adult life. So, get real about your fear, and step into ... FREEDOM.

G ... GUILT. Most of us create THIS out of nothing. The should ofs, could ofs, would ofs ... all that stuff has no power. It drains us of the good things. Flip it to GRATITUDE, and be thankful for each experience. Why not?

H ... Humiliation is an attack on our entire being and is used by many people in power, such as parents over children, teachers over students, bosses over employees, police over speeders, and so on. Humiliation affects the thymus gland. If it continues, it may cause thyroid problems. Plus, it raises hell with your self-esteem. It needs to change—not the quality of humiliation but your reaction to it. Change it to HONOUR. Honour yourself for who you are to stay well.

I ... INJURED. Living in old wounds or stuck in the past. You must recognize it to own it and decide whether you wish to remain where you are. If not, try to figure out what value you received out of the injury. It may be just to be aware that you don't injure anyone else in the same way. Get involved, and change the injury stance to INVOLVEMENT. Don't let it keep you procrastinating; move forward.

J . . . JUDGEMENT. It's so easy to make snap judgments. We do it even without all the necessary information. However, even with all the information, do we really have the right to judge anyone? No judgment means you have flipped it to JOY.

K . . . KNOW IT ALL. Some people must have an opinion on every-thing and try to make themselves "right." Most people have been made wrong so often, and therein lies the rationale for the need to be "right." To change this stance, you need to relinquish your need to be right all the time. Do it out of KINDNESS, simply by saying, "You are right." This terminates a lot of tug-o-wars.

L . . . LAZY. Change takes a lot of work. Consequently, most of us live in a "make it easy" scenario. We become lazy. Do the work. and become an involved LEADER instead.

M . . . MANIPULATION out of fear may create a false sense of security. Not wanting to change or do anything out of the ordinary keeps things as they are and familiar. This tactic is used by parents, partners, bosses, clergy, and teachers. Such approaches get people to do what is desired. To flip this, you must dig into your own "creation box." Rather than have others do your dance, you must MANIFEST your own outcome by becoming centred, perhaps through MEDITATION. The result will be that you will no longer require others to do your bidding.

N . . . NUMBING. Many things occur in our lives that seem to be unbearable with no answer as to why circumstances happen as they do. Consequently, simply numbing out can be an easy way of avoiding the situation. There are many ways to produce this reaction. Doctors will prescribe medication, friends will say, "Just don't think about it" or "It will take time." No one wishes to talk about it or hear about it, so numbing out becomes the way to be. When my life partner died, numbing out looked like the only way to survive. However, I chose to face the situa-tion, stay in the moment, and face the indescribable pain, loss, loneliness, and fear. Staying in the NOW is all we have. Being present is the end of the process. I feel a lot stronger and willing to move on.

O . . . OPPRESSION is used globally against people of different races, colour, beliefs, sex, women, children, and so on. It has been passed down from generation to generation. It has become part of who we are. Oppression is so subtle that we hardly recognize that we are in its clutches. Most people don't want to admit it, but even the oppressed become the oppressors. One can only stop it by speaking against it and moving to ONENESS. The flip is to accept without judgment and with love that we are all one.

P . . . PETTINESS. It is so easy to point the finger, do the "look," and be rude. Most of us have been there. It is part of gossip, put-downs, and snide remarks. In a word, it's PETTINESS. What would happen if we just quit it and refused to be part of other people's pettiness, or called each other on pettiness in a good and kind way? This would result in being POWERFUL and provide opportunities to enjoy better lives. Try it.

Q . . . QUITTING. When life is tough, you may simply give up for some reason, like "it's easier to give up" or "not risking." Quitting can be positive or negative, depending on what it involves. For example, quitting the use of substances (pills, drugs, booze) is considered good. In the process of quitting, QUESTIONING your process and objectives provides an avenue to move forward in a positive sense. Seeking information in your questioning process leads to more positive decisions. What truly works for you and moves you into a better space? The more questions you ask yourself and others the better. Be honest with yourself, and the most productive awareness will come from you.

R . . . RESENTMENT. Sometimes bad things occur in our lives. Most of us have learned that holding a grudge may turn into RESENTMENT. As long as we keep resenting, it will stop us from moving forward in a good way. To flip resentment, we must learn to forgive. Some things may appear to be difficult to forgive. Consequently, we may become bitter and lose RESPECT, primarily for ourselves. As long as we hold resentments, we continually give up our power. When powerless, we build up more resentment and then blame, and eventually, we get lost in the turmoil. Dig into your self-RESPECT, and forgive yourself for your resentments.

S . . . SETTLING. The majority of us do not explore enough. If the status quo dictates, "Do it," we do it, most of the time settling for less. Settling for less stems from seeing yourself as stupid or unworthy. Consequently, we just take what comes along or do what someone tells us to do. Part of this is also laziness. We live in a time where everything is made easy. If not, we don't accept it. I implore you to do your work. We say things like, "I'm not ready yet" or "The timing is off." As a result, we settle for less. How do we change this? Stop being lazy. Stop looking for a way outside yourself. Stop SETTLING. Take inventory, and see if you are being all you can be. Stop procrastinating! Start listening to your inner voice (gut feeling). Trust that feelings, and act immediately without question. After all, who other than you knows what is best for you? Putting the inevitable on the back burner only opens you up to illness, loneliness, and depression. So . . . STOP, listen, and love.

T . . . TEMPER TANTRUM. Many of you will not want to own this one. A friend of mine said he never wanted children, because his dad had a bad temper, as he did, and he did not wish to pass on that gene. I had to smile and say to myself, "It's not genes; it's not getting your own way." This is called a TEMPER TANTRUM. Temper tantrums are a great way to control, manipulate, and instil fear, but most of all, to get our own way. Some tantrums are quieter, taking the form of pouting or the silent treatment. Changing this habit is relatively easy. Simply envision a little child throwing him or herself on the floor, screaming and kicking. That is what you are doing. See yourself needing to be right. Just be kind, and let someone else be right. You will find that it's quite easy. TRUST the process. Given time and practice, you do not have to blame anyone. You do not have to be right all the time. Trust yourself most of all, that you are capable of change and happiness.

U . . . UNDESERVING. "Oh no, I couldn't, I'm not educated enough . . . it takes brains for that." These expressions are ways of saying "I'm not good enough" or "I'm UNDESERVING." It comes from not being able to see your real gifts. Perhaps you were put down at some point in your life, and that tape keeps playing. "I'm not smart enough. I'm not good enough." This tape will continue playing until you are willing to see that you are not more or less of a person than anyone else but amazing in your own UNIQUENESS. Don't yearn to be like someone else; be you. Don't try to be better than anyone else; just be you. Here is a little exercise to get started. Every time you look in a mirror, regard yourself as unique and say, "You are special/gifted/amazing" or whatever positive words you can think of. In fourteen days or less, you will experience a noticeable shift away from the underserving attitudes you may have harboured.

V . . . VICTIM. We are all VICTIMS of someone or something. We may have been the victim of our parents, teachers, pastors, government, or legal system. We may act like a victim to be noticed or heard or to elicit pity from others. Take a look at what you get out of playing the victim card. You may say, "Nothing." Well, if you weren't getting something out of it, you wouldn't be doing it. We remain in victim mode, because it provides a payoff. Those who do not play it anymore have stopped being victimized, are consciously VOICING what happened, then letting go and moving on to their dreams. By voicing your truth, you can no longer be victimized. The only thing you must be aware of is to not become the victimizer. Consequently, you must deal with your anger and put it away. Yes, you can do it. Validate that you are capable of anything toward which you apply your mind and your heart.

W . . . WHINE. Don't you just hate it when adults whine? I don't know about you, but I can't stand it, and have to leave the room or say something, such as, "Stop your damn whining." I believe it stems from not being heard or listened to as a child. Then we bring it into our adult lives. Does it work for you? If you live with a whiner and you are a whiner, perhaps it does. All I know it is extremely irritating. What's the flip? You are all grown up now, so it's time you became the WITNESS. It's time you began to see and hear and not judge. Know by your presence and perceptions that you get what you ask for. Be the true witness, and give gratitude.

X . . . X marks the spot. Put all your intentions, desires, wishes, and dreams to the flip side of how to be and live in the A to Z way of being.

Y . . . YOU are the boss of your life. You now can choose to change from simply surviving to living in the present.

Z . . . a ZEST for living should ensue with a conscious flip of negative terms to more positive ways of living your life.

CHAPTER 6

THE POWER

Happiness is an inside job.
Don't assign anyone else that much power over you.
—Anonymous

Who has the power? The first one to come to mind is me. Really! Every excuse you make for not living your dream is power given up to someone or something else. No one can take your power unless you let them. They can use trickery, bullying, humiliation, or any other ploy you can think of, but they can't take your power unless you give it up.

If your power is up for grabs, someone will take it; I guarantee it. So, let's see what being in your power looks like. It doesn't mean you hold anyone else's power by overpowering them or that you're smarter than anyone. You don't need a lot of power either. You can be in you power in a really good way with a big smile and a kind word or kind action. Being in your power encourages others to seek and be in theirs.

The absence of fear keeps the power suckers out of your life. So, if you know what fear looks and feels like, then stepping out of it won't be as difficult as we are made to believe. Remember, almost all fear is unreal, something made up to keep us powerless.

A dear friend had some health issues. He was experiencing some angina pain and asked his doctor for some pain medication. He believed in western medications and took a lot of prescriptions. He had beaten cancer and seemed relatively okay. Long story short, he was put on morphine, which kept him numb. Eventually, he became suicidal. He was rushed to the hospital, where they took him off morphine. He seemed to be somewhat "out to lunch." The attending doctor wrote on his chart that he had dementia. He did not have dementia; he was suffering from withdrawal. However, because of his behaviour, they tied him to the bed, creating panic and fear. He reacted by yelling and demanding to know what was happening. Hospital staff said he was belligerent and moved him to a room with no windows. He didn't know day from night. In my opinion, they were punishing him and preventing him from recovering. His wife and I tried to have him moved, but by the time that happened, he was so weak and run down that going home was not an option. His heart did not mend, and he became less willing to fight to regain his health. He passed away shortly thereafter.

My mother once overdosed on medication, and we almost lost her. Thank God she ended up in a different community, where she fell ill, and the doctor there said she was taking way too much medication and cut her prescription in half. She recovered and started asking questions of the other doctor, who had been so willing to prescribe. The reason I am relating these stories is to indicate how easy it is to relinquish your power, which can ultimately end your life. Consequently, in any situation, be cautious, and don't automatically give up your power. Be cognisant of what is going on. Hold on to your power.

I was taught to believe that a doctor was right. After all, he was educated in these matters. My experience has shown that this is not necessarily so. A doctor told me I had diabetes and was going to prescribe me pills. I said no; I don't take any form of pills. The next doctor looked at my chart and also said I had diabetes. I demanded a full test for diabetes. The results were negative: no diabetes. So, take your power back. Exercise and eat well, and don't forget to ask lots of questions when you are confronted with similar circumstances. Hold on to your power.

There is another place where we surrender our power. If someone makes you angry and you react, they have your power. Stay balanced, smile, and say, "This does not fit for me, and I choose to stay in my power." (Blow off steam later, if need be.)

Our society encourages anger. We like it and approve of it so much that we have anger-management courses. We use anger to gain power over others. Many people are afraid of anger, primarily their own. Think of the positive consequences if all such anger could be managed and supplanted to an inconsequential emotion.

Even the word "power" or "powerful" instils an element of fear. Considering the most powerful countries in the world can ignite a feeling of fear. Fear keeps us from our own unique self and away from our power. We need to create the life we want and step back into our own power.

Education, or lack thereof, are both about power and fear. We send our little people to teaching institutions at around age four. Why? Because someone said it was a good idea. In my opinion, they were wrong. At four years old, these children are still babies in need of Mom and Dad to support, love, and teach them. When did it become okay to give our little ones to a system that most adults would not tolerate? I'm not sure how this empowers our children. Next time you drop off or pick up your child from school, look into the eyes of all the children, and see how powerless they appear.

Obey the rules, or else. This means you have no power and little to say or do about it. If your child breaks a rule, the system lets you know. Often, they have had their say, and then you get your say. Make sure your child has a say. Be their advocate, and help them retain their power. I am not saying make the teacher wrong, because that would mean blame, and in blame, we also give up power.

There is a false sense of power out there that keeps most of the world in crisis . . . the struggle for it . . . the fear of not having it . . . striving to meet the status quo. The law instils a sense of powerlessness. There is an abundance of laws, with most not making too much sense and not fitting everyone. The Church has power over the "flock," with most people following blindly to who knows where. One religion makes the next one wrong in many eyes. There are judgments if you do not adhere to all the rules. You can belong, or you can't belong, or you can belong, but you must change to be like the flock, or your power will be stripped.

A friend of mine, Aaron, struggled most of his young life to fit into a religion that made him feel bad and wrong. When he stepped into his power and came out, telling people he was gay, the church, his parents, and his siblings turned their backs on him. Nice Christian behaviour, yes? What a way to try and keep him powerless. He remains in his power and is happy. If the church you go to talks about love but supports the judgement of others, you need to see how they became so powerful that you are willing to bow to their power.

Families . . . bless them and all the rules it takes to belong to one. Who made the family so powerful that breaking away becomes a near-death experience if you do not conform to the rules with which you grew up? When I came out and moved away, one of my sisters called and said I was a coward and had destroyed the family name, and they all wished I was dead. I did not get angry or debate the situation. I simply said, "I choose to stay in my power, and please, if you feel this way, please never call me again." She hasn't. Neither has the rest of my family.

If you were in your power, what would look like? You would not need to compete with anyone. Comparing yourself to others would be a thing of the past. Anger would be almost non-existent. So would making others wrong, so you can be right. Selling out to fit into a club or group wouldn't happen. You would realize that you fit everywhere no matter what. People pleasing would not be a chore; it would simply happen. You would probably do only the job you love and sing out loud while doing it. Your smile would be contagious, with others wondering what you have been up to. You would speak to everyone. Your light would shine, so little children would stare at you. Dogs would probably wag their tails. Fear would be put in its rightful place, and love would be abundant. Being in your own power means never having to overpower anyone else. Consequently, if that is not an issue for you, freedom gets closer and closer.

You would be more accepting of others and let the past stay where it belongs, in the past. However, you could still go there without denial or giving up your power. You would live in the moment all the time.

Smile . . . really smile. It takes more facial muscles to frown than to smile. My dog, Diva, somehow figured out how to smile. It makes everyone who witnesses her smile also break into a smile. That's how it works.

CHAPTER 7

WORKING IT

Fighting your ego is a melodrama of the ego.
—Deepak Chopra

"It's never going to be perfect." That's what I said when I started writing this book. "No one will buy it. I'm not a writer. I'm not smart enough or good enough." I had a chat with my little pot-bellied ego and said, "Fuck off, I'm doing it." Then I picked up a pen and started to write. If you are reading this now, my ego was wrong, and that's how I like it.

The ego comes at us in so many ways, it's often difficult to keep up with it. So, I am asking you to become really aware of your ego, so you can challenge it until it gives up on you. You must challenge it continuously, because even when you think you've got it under control, surprise . . . there it is again.

I see my ego as a little pot-bellied muscle man who, when I am unsure, appears from under my shirt collar and stands on my shoulder and starts his little routine. He can be so nice that it almost gets me at times. He can also play the victim and incite pity, or he can become a bully and get me to call on my anger. My little ego man is a trickster, or am I the trickster, just playing a role? I ask myself who is calling the shots now, in this moment—me or him? If I can stay truthful to myself, it is mostly him. I flick him off my shoulder and say, "Ego be gone." I hear him hit the floor and grumble, but he always comes back. I will even flick him in public. No one notices, because their little egos have them wrapped up in their past and their fears of what others may be thinking about them. I realize that no one really sees my little flaws, because they are too worried about their own. That's the ego at work. So, whenever you are stuck in the past or waiting until morning and planning, that's when your ego is running the show.

Fear . . . I've already written about. It is all done in the ego, because 99 percent of our fears are unreal, created by our ego to prevent us from encountering new experiences. Change is difficult, because up until now, your ego has been in control. "Every step you take, every breath you take, I'll be on you, because you belong to me." That's your ego's song.

Making excuses is another thing most of us do without even thinking. I was made very aware of all the excuses I was making in my life when I read a book called *Excuses be Gone* by Dr. Wayne Dyer. I encourage everyone to read this book. It will put a dent in your ego's helmet. It will also open doors for you that maybe you thought would never open.

I was doing an empowerment workshop with about thirty people, including teachers, lawyers, leaders, and a minister. In one morning, I kept tabs on how many excuses people used to stay in familiar places, even if they were unhealthy and unsafe. I counted 327 different excuses, and everyone spoke of them as if they were real. Most people defended their excuses, especially if they were about family. Change takes work, not hard work, just "working it" at a conscious level all the time. If you can see the humour in it, make a game of it. Do it with a friend or spouse, and have fun. It becomes a new consciousness or a new way of being.

Blame is yet another way of remaining in a familiar place. As long as it is someone else's fault, you get to stay the same. Bad things happen to good people, so get used to it. However, if you can get around it, ask how the bad situation was created, own your part in it (if you had a part), learn from it, and give thanks that you made it, even if your ego didn't want you to. You will be able to move forward in a good way toward your pursuit of happiness.

Denial, pretending, and lying are other ways to halt change. To work this, you have to be honest with yourself and about the events that have taken place in your life, including from whence the rules came that keep you quiet. Remember, you are here for a good time. My friend, Harold, from the first time I met him as a teen (he was a neighbour) would come and hang out, play, check out second-hand stores with me, go for ice cream, and so on. My partner would always say, "It must be nice that you can play all day while I work." He was part of our play and didn't even know it.

When you wake up in the morning, even if it's difficult, smile. See the new day. Jump to it like it's the last day of your life, and live it to the fullest. Be kind to at least one person each day. Call them, go see them, just do it. Find time to be still and know who you are and that your spirit is with you, always wanting to meet your dream.

Here is an exercise. It may be difficult for some, but if you can stick with it, you should see a major shift in your life. For the next fourteen days, don't complain, not even in your thoughts. Even after four days, you will note a shift. You will be surprised at how much complaining you do. Work it.

Learn to meditate. People have been doing it for thousands of years, and they can't all be wrong. There are many ways to do it. Silence, mantras, music, guided imagery, praying, chanting, and drumming all work. Meditation is not about stopping all thought, which is impossible. It is about finding the gap between thoughts and putting your desires and dreams in the gaps to the universe. Try it; what have you got to lose? Work it.

Yoga is another old practice I have just started. I'm not entirely sure how it works, but again, the masters of many thousands of years can't all be wrong. All I know right now is "ouch," but I am working it.

Take a walk, and be with nature. I find it one of the best ways to start my day. It doesn't hurt your body. Try a short walk. Walk a block. I am sure something good will happen. Work it.

There are all sorts of little sayings out there, such as "Happiness is a state of mind," and "Smile and the world smiles with you." If any of these work for you, use them. Work it.

Working it means change. Risk a bit. Try something new. Meet someone new. You can do it. You can have all the information in the world, read every self-help book on the market, know every diet, think about it all, set time limits and so on, but if you don't do anything with all these goodies, it is all useless information. Push yourself to change. Believe me, breaking the routine may be all you need to create what you want.

You can do it on your own; you don't need someone to hold your hand or encourage you. Go and have a chat with "you." Kick your ego in the butt. You have the power. Work it.

CHAPTER 8

A WAY – THE BEGINNING

New beginnings are often disguised as painful endings.
—Lau Tzu

If we stay in the moment, it will always be brand new. We tend to hear it spoken a lot . . . "Just stay in the moment." This is difficult to do when your past generates thoughts, rules, and beliefs. They keep popping up in the moment, saying things like, "Ah . . . you must not forget where you came from and who you are. You must not forget what she/he/they did. Be on your guard at all times, and be careful who you trust. Most people want something from you. Be careful. Don't trust strangers." Staying in the moment? Yeah right. With all this going on in your mind? Every second is a new beginning. Really. The last one is now in the past, and you can't do anything about it.

If only we could stay in the moment. However, our ego likes us confused and in the power of yesterday or tomorrow. To do that, the ego must keep the moment confusing, so we never get to our real power or happiness. A new way of being requires change from how you are now to a life lived free of the shadow of fear and the ego, basking in light and love.

I know you have the awareness. I know you came to this place knowing how to be. I don't doubt for a moment that you are perfect, whole, and complete in every way. I know that you have brought certain people into your life for a reason. I believe everything happens for a reason—I'm just not always sure what that reason is. However, in the long run, this reason often reveals itself.

The hard times are made harder by clinging to old beliefs and fears. You can change that. Make a choice. Lean on me or someone else. Cry if you need to; it is one of the best releases. Scream out loud about the injustices in the world. Get on the ten o'clock news, and help wake up the world, if that's your purpose. Know your intentions at all times, but most of all, seek true happiness. Don't let it pass you by because of faulty beliefs, self-imposed moral rules, or fears. It is possible. Too many people say, "I can't do anything about the world. I can't change it; it's too big. So, I'll just do my thing and whatever happens, happens." Making a shift in your life and acting it out for the world to see will cause a ripple effect on others. You may not see it or hear about it, but if you are doing it in a good way, I guarantee it is moving someone else.

A perfect world. Wouldn't it be grand? When I walk in the forest and all is still, I know it is possible if there is no greed, hate, taxes, or fear. It's where/what you feel. What is, is. You can experience peace and love. So, I thought I would take a small survey and ask a number of people the following question: if they could create a perfect world, what would it look like? I didn't give them time to think long on it, just straight from the heart. This is what they said.

A scientist in his late sixties said that as soon as he heard the question, he thought of the song "Imagine" by John Lennon.

I asked a ten-year-old. Her reply was that we shouldn't have to die. She had lost her grandmother recently. She went on to say life should be happy, and there should be no wars.

A school teacher of twenty-six years said she sees that the world has shifted, and she thinks people forget that they need one another. So, for her it would be people genuinely and emotionally attached to one another to create a new generation that would be more aware of what truly matters.

A grade one class was asked the same question. It was incredible what they came up with.

...not killing animals for food

...no littering AT ALL

. . . don't say mean words

. . . everyone would be kind

. . . no wars

. . . no arguments

. . . no killing

. . . lots of trees, bushes, and leaves

. . . don't hurt anybody

. . . grow your own fruits and vegetables

. . . don't cut down as many trees

. . . don't waste paper

. . . don't waste water

. . . don't waste power

. . . exercise more

. . . everybody has fun

. . . no fighting in my family

. . . don't waste food

. . . don't do anything mean to family

. . . be good for Mom and Dad

. . . take care of your family

From the mouth of babes comes some real truths . . . I love it.

Shirley, a hairdresser for over twenty years who has seen and heard a lot, says in a perfect world, we would let go of fear, anxiety, and stress and create a life of fun and laughter. And . . . there has to be lots of love.

I asked Ronny the same question, and without hesitation he said sparkly, twinkly, a bright light aura of happiness and smiles.

Ben said no hunger . . . good, free, health care . . . peace, love, and honesty.

I asked a small business owner. She said her perfect world was the way it is now, with perhaps a little less confrontation. She added a caveat, however, saying she was having a good day, and she keeps her head in the sand a lot.

Fifteen-year-old Becca said no wars . . . no hate . . . everyone was happy.

If we can think it and feel it, then we should be able to do it. Every response from people of all ages could, if fact, happen . . . except for no dying. Maybe we need to create a batch of new leaders who are not focussed on power and greed. Leaders who will take seriously the possibility of world peace.

We are a throw-away society. We waste enough food and goods to take care of three worlds. There is no excuse for homelessness, hunger, or welfare. Our elders need much better care. Go sit in your child's classroom, and see what they are learning. If you don't like it, change it.

Stand up for our sake, and encourage others to stand with you. The squeaky wheel gets the grease. Today, no one wants to be "the one." If you are "the one," call me, and I will make a noise with you. Something has to change. We must take back our power from the powers that be and create a life of harmony, where all is well. I challenge you to put down your weapons of anger, hate, revenge, and regret and pick up your flag of peace and love to create some happiness. Don't forget to hold on to those magic moments. There is good everywhere . . . acknowledge it.

The beginning starts now.

NOTES

NOTES

NOTES

NOTES

About the Author

Richard Dolen was born in Calgary, Alberta, Canada, and raised in a small rural community, with his family trying to scratch a living on a local dirt farm. He is Métis and a registered member of the Métis Nation of British Columbia, Canada.

Through the eyes of poverty, hatred, and discrimination, he developed overwhelming feelings of guilt, shame, and self-hatred. By the time Richard turned six, he had lost hearing in one ear, was labelled slow in school, and had been sexually abused. He also suffers from dyslexia. Suicide often entered his mind as a method to stop the pain.

His family was Roman Catholic, which played a significant role in his future aspirations to help those suffering from many of society's ills. He had first-hand knowledge of the now-openly discussed topic of sexual abuse in the Church. He was an altar boy and abused. He left home at age fifteen, seeking a better life than what he had been dealt for the first fifteen years. After living in societies where being Métis or First Nations were looked down upon, Richard soon realized that many of society's ills evolved from addictions, family violence, family secrets, physical and sexual abuse, alcohol and drug abuse, and feelings of inadequacy. The fact he was Métis was a family secret, never spoken of openly in the family circle. He suffered from years of severe family dysfunction.

As an adult, he became a life-skills coach, working in suicide prevention, and helping those who struggled with alcoholism, violence in the home, and virtually every form of addiction suffered by desperate men and women. He began running groups in transition houses in California for young adolescents and realized there must be a better way to help people who descend into such debilitating hopelessness.

Richard felt he could help those who had lost their way by providing workshops dedicated to encouraging participants to face their fears, develop self-confidence, and move beyond the quagmire of depression, fear, and physical/emotional torment.

CPSIA information can be obtained
at www.ICGtesting.com
Printed in the USA
LVOW11s1706280418
575060LV00003B/9/P